Common Sense Solutions for Success

● ● ● ● ● ● ● ● ●

YOUR GUIDE TO A HAPPIER, MORE PRODUCTIVE,
MORE SUCCESSFUL LIFE!

by G. Eric Gordon

L E G A C Y   B O O K S

Arlington, Texas

■Legacy Books
One Arlington Centre
1112 East Copeland Road, Fifth Floor
Arlington, Texas 76011

Common Sense Solutions for Success
Copyright © 1997 by G. Eric Gordon

Printed in the United States of America
01 00 99 98 97 010 5 4 3 2 1

ISBN 1-56530-254-0
Cover photo by Mary Ann Sherman,
2032 Farrington St., Dallas, TX 75207

Cover design by Dennis Davidson
Page design by Michael Melton

Common Sense Solutions for Success

Barbara!

Go out & Succeed!

This book is for common people with
extraordinary dreams.

It is dedicated to the loving memory of
Thelma and Prinest Carter

I also want to thank my mother
Ms. Amy Gordon
and my wife
Dorothea
for their continued support.

To my sons Elijah and Noah and my brothers
Larry, Dar, Bruce, and Kell-Rock:
I LOVE YOU GUYS!!

A very special thank you goes to
Ms. Gwendolyn James
who believed in me before I believed in myself!

Contents

Preface

● ● ● ● ● ● ● ● ● ●

I don't know why we do it. Why do so many of us make things harder than they should be? We are born skeptics. We are told over and over that nothing comes easy, life is hard, don't expect too much—you'll be disappointed!

Of course, there is some truth to these statements. We often have to work very hard to achieve our goals; but why do so many of us feel that true success and happiness are nothing more than a fantasy? The vast majority of Americans will never realize their full potential! Why? Because we don't believe that the good things in life can really be ours!

Well, my friends, I am here to announce and proclaim to the world that you really can have the things you truly desire in life, and getting it is easier than you know! Let me put it this way. Anything in life that you truly value can be yours!! Naturally, this book will show you how to get it. It's easier than you think.

The reason I started my own consulting firm and wrote this book was to help bring the word of power and self-fulfillment to others. I call this book *Common Sense Solutions for Success* because the steps you must take to have a happier, more prosperous life are simple steps that have been around since the beginning of recorded history! Most importantly for all of us, any person with drive and average intelligence can achieve tremendous results in his or her life! The information in this book is not magic, but the success strategies can work like magic if consistently applied to every area in life!

Why This Book?

It's sad, but the great majority of Americans don't have a clue when it comes to achieving success in life. Most really don't believe that wealth, prosperity, financial independence, and happiness can be attained through our own actions. Many believe instead that one must inherit money, know the right people, be some kind of entertainer/athlete, or win the lottery—good luck. It is this belief that leaves most people willing to settle for a nice, comfortable life of mediocrity. We just don't believe that it can happen to us!

This Is Why This Book Is for You!

We hear it all the time—why something won't work! I am in the same boat. Before this book was published, I submitted it to many publishers. They all turned it down. Heck, I was even turned down by literary agents. Even the people who finally published this book had their doubts. The vice president of marketing had concerns about why people would buy this book. She said that life was hard, and she wasn't sure the message would be received and valued by you (the public)!! But here it is, and it provides a great lesson for those of you who are born skeptics! The first and most critical components to attaining your dreams are faith, courage, and the determination NOT to listen to all the naysayers in the world! Stick to your guns and go get what you want!!

This book provides a solid, clear road map for the attainment of your goals. Each of us possesses certain skills. Whether these skills are enhanced or begin to fade depends upon us. We will help you use your God-given talents for high achievement. Here's how it works:

YOUR FOUNDATION: Beliefs, values, self-esteem, and vision.

- ★ THOUGHTS: We create our own reality based upon our thoughts. We are the way we think!

- ★ ACTIONS: The manifestation of thought. Our actions show the world how and what we think about.

- ★ HABITS: Those activities that support and enhance our ability to truly excel in life. Our habits allow us to do more—or could cause us to lose what little we have.

This book will address each area, and will help you tie them together in a package of activities working to bring you what you desire or value most in life! This will be one of the most exciting books you have ever read!

This Book Has the Answers You're Looking For

No matter what your profession, educational level, race, or current social status, this book has exciting answers for you. Here's what you'll learn:

★ How to understand/identify your life mission (or purpose).

★ How to enhance your self-esteem and confidence.

★ How to create an exciting vision for your life!

★ How to recognize your value and build solid professional and personal relationships.

★ How to stay positive and persevere when the going gets rough!

★ How to eliminate self-imposed limitations that have held you back.

★ How to gain a tremendous advantage over any competitor, in any situation.

You'll find the success journey to be so exciting and so stimulating that you will often forget that your efforts are supposed to be work! You have made your decision. That decision says that you want, desire, and expect to achieve more of the good things life has to offer! Enjoy this book. I hope that you feel the excitement and enthusiasm that engulfed me when I was writing it. If you yield to the advice, I guarantee that you'll be on your way to more than you've ever hoped for.

What Is Success?

● ● ● ● ● ● ● ● ●

The lessons you are about to learn will provide you with knowledge of those success traits and habits you'll need to be a high achiever in life. This book will show you how to enjoy the good life! You will know the secrets of developing a success mentality. You will turn failures into tools for future successes. You will learn through your most powerful asset—your mind—how to become virtually unstoppable. The world is at your fingertips. You really can fulfill your dreams and lead a successful life. It won't always be easy, but if you remain faithful and focused, success is yours!

The name of this book is *Common Sense Solutions for Success.* Many people say they want to be successful and want a successful life, but how does one know when it has been attained? What is success? Who decides what success is? How is it measured?

There are no easy answers to these questions. So, our first order of business is to discuss the characteristics of success and examine how you will know when you have attained it.

1

Webster's New World Dictionary defines *success* as: 1. a favorable result 2. the gaining of wealth, fame, etc. *Successful* is defined as: 1. turning out as was hoped for 2. having gained wealth, fame, etc.

According to Webster, *success* is directly related to gaining wealth and fame. *Successful* is having things turn out as hoped for. Is having things turn out as hoped for another way of saying that one has achieved one's goals? Is achieving wealth or fame your goal? Is Webster's definition an appropriate description of success for you?

The late Vince Lombardi, legendary Super Bowl coach of the Green Bay Packers, once said:

> The difference between the successful person and others is not lack of strength, not lack of knowledge, but rather a lack of will.

Does having a strong will lead to success? If so, why and how? What does this mean to you?

Your Mission Is the Key

Success means something different to every human being. It depends on one's values, feelings, beliefs, and attitudes toward life. To determine what success means to you, first ask yourself, "What do I value most in life?"

A person's definition of success depends on how that person has decided to live his or her life in accordance with those things he/she values. If, for example, a person's goal in life was to live on a tropical island, that person will feel that he or she has achieved success when he/she can live life the way he/she envisioned it. This simply means that success is based on a person's ability to achieve what he/she feels is most important in life! Usually, those achievements relate to a person's life mission or purpose.

The idea of success is subjective and will vary with each individual. End of discussion, right? Not quite. Let's examine the concept of "life mission" more closely. For example, if a man's lifelong dream was to never work again and he achieved that dream by losing his job and becoming a homeless person, could we say this man has achieved success? Probably not! Why? Because, in the process of achieving this goal, he has surrendered total control of his life! If that man achieved his goal of not working by becoming a homeless person, here's what could happen to him:

He must now...

★ depend on others for food and shelter
★ subject himself to the rules of any shelter he stays in
★ often endure harsh weather conditions
★ understand that his options are now very limited, at best!

What price has this person paid, and was it worth it? There's more to success than being able to do as we please. Decisions yield outcomes. From these out-comes, each of us determines our own success. Here are the traits I normally attribute to a successful person (or one who is living a successful life):

★ Has identified and is living his/her life mission
★ Has greater control over his/her life and its circum-stances
★ Has the power to do as he/she pleases
★ Has the means (money) to enjoy the material things life offers
★ Is relaxed and happy with the path he/she has chosen
★ Enjoys his/her life and all that it brings
★ Is relaxed and at peace with him/herself and with life
★ Has the will and power to change any aspect of life that is displeasing or is not consistent his/her ideal self or vision.

Each person is placed on this earth to fulfill a purpose. We all have talents in some area of life. This purpose, or mission, is your divine calling. Identifying and knowing your purpose increases your chances for achieving suc-cess. Why? Because your mission will be the driving force behind your efforts. Your mission compels you to live up to your greatest potential! It provides direction for the special talents and skills each of us possesses.

Finding Your Mission

Do you know your life mission? Most of us have never considered what our life mission could be. This is one reason so many talented and educated people fail to live up to their potential.

If you want to know your life mission, just do one simple thing—THINK ABOUT IT! Your first assignment is to determine what's important to you. What do you value most in life? Find time each day to just relax and think about what you truly want out of life. Ask yourself:

★ What do I want most from life?
★ What do I believe in?
★ What are the three most important things to me?
★ What three things do I value most in life?
★ What activities give me the greatest amount of pleasure?
★ If I could have (or do) anything in the world, what would I want?

My life mission is to help others achieve their life mission! If I can help people live up to their highest potential, I will consider my life a success!

Your life mission may be similar to mine, or it may not, but whatever it is, this book can help you achieve it.

Success Is Important

Oddly enough, most of us hardly think about what is really important to us. Most of us sit around hoping that something will happen to improve our lives. Dennis Kimbro, author of *Think and Grow Rich—A Black Choice*, mentioned a two-year study written by psychologist William Marsten. In this study, Dr. Marsten asked three thousand individuals, "What have you to live for?" Amazingly, 94 percent of those surveyed had no definite answer for this question, to which Dennis Kimbro correctly concluded that 94 percent of those surveyed had no definite purpose. Can the general public be much different? I doubt it.

This helps explain why so many people have yet to live up to their fullest potential. How can a person really be successful if he or she is unsure of what he/she can do or wants to do? Most people don't know where, or how, to begin.

So wake up! Get into life. Find out what's really important to you and get after it! Build a burning fire of desire within yourself and watch how good things begin to happen for you! Your mission may become an exciting force behind your efforts!

Success is many things to many people, but one fact is clear. Success, or lack of it, is a direct reflection of you. Your level of achievement tells the world how you feel about yourself and the type of life you feel you deserve.

There Are Winners and Losers

In the game of life there are "winners" and "losers." The rules of the game have been established, though at times, they aren't always fair. Les Brown once said, "Life isn't fair. Life just is!" Those who achieve their goals, even when things are not perfect, or when faced with obstacles and setbacks, are winners in life. So, begin setting your sights on what you really desire from life, and build a determination to get it. As you will learn from this book, it's always up to you!

Do you have what it takes to be successful, to be a winner? I think you do, so let's get started!

Your Foundation
Vision of Self
● ● ● ● ● ● ● ● ●

So where does it really begin for high achievers? I believe our lives can be built, just as houses are built. As with any house, a solid foundation is necessary if the house is to stand solidly for years. We build our lives exactly the same way, with a foundation of beliefs that affect everything that we do or achieve.

Anyone who has ever achieved any level of success first had to *believe* in his or her capacity to do it. These people had to believe themselves to be smart, capable, competent, and determined enough to achieve their goals. Our foundation of beliefs determines how high we desire to rise, or how low we'll allow ourselves to go. It's something no person can run away from.

From our beliefs, we create our self-image, and our lives reflect those thoughts and the image. So our first challenge is to make sure that we have a strong belief in our abilities, and that our image, or vision, reflects those beliefs. Once a person creates the vision of his/her *ideal self* firmly in mind, that person has taken the first step toward attainment of that vision!!

It will amaze you just how quickly your life begins to change the minute you clearly see and know what you want to do and be! You are, and always will be, the way you see yourself!! Believe it or not, the vision you have of yourself and of your future will come true. *Even now, you are developing habits, either good or bad, to ensure that it will happen.* Look at your life now: Aren't you about where you believed you would be? *We either rise or fall to the level of our own expectations—our vision!*

This is vitally important as you prepare for your success journey. To achieve any level of success, you must create a successful vision according to what success means to you. Then you must believe yourself worthy of success, and most importantly, see yourself in possession of that which you desire!

Each of us creates an image of ourselves within our own minds, and in time, we become that image! As you think about the picture you have of yourself, remember that *your ability to achieve good things is directly related to your vision.* Start right away to create an exciting and successful image of yourself. Begin with the basics. First of all, *like yourself!*

Then begin to:

★ See yourself as worthy of success and good fortune
★ See yourself as a winner
★ See yourself in possession of your identified goal(s)
★ See yourself as a competent person who gets things done.

In the book of Mark 11:24, Jesus said:

Therefore I say unto you, What things soever ye desire, when ye pray, believe that ye receive them and ye shall have them.

You can have the things you desire if you can believe and see yourself already in possession of it.

So solidify your foundation by creating a powerful and exciting vision of yourself. Here are a few things to begin visualizing. Where do you see yourself five to ten years from now? What will you be doing? Where will you live? What kind of house will you live in? What will be your income? What kind of people will you associate with?

Steps for Creating a Winning Vision

The person who can see himself or herself making a million dollars has already taken the first step toward the accomplishment of that goal. Success is not an accident. Those who achieve it do so because they believe that they deserve it and can see themselves in possession of it.

Once you begin to see yourself having the success you want, the powers of your mind (both your conscious and subconscious minds) will instantly begin working to bring that mental picture into reality. Your vision triggers the success mechanisms within your mind and directs your thoughts and actions toward your vision. Remember—your mind will not let you visualize that which you cannot attain. Napoleon Hill said it best when he stated, "*Anything the mind of man can conceive (visualize) and believe, it can achieve.*"

Here are two exercises you can do. The first helps you develop a positive frame of mind with which to create your vision. It provides verbal support that serves to enhance your visualization process. It's called self-talk and affirmations. The second exercise is the process of visualization.

1) **Self-Talk/Affirmations:** Our minds react to external stimuli, such as sight and sound. Our self-image is a direct result of what we've heard from others and what we say to ourselves! However, we can create positive images for our future by simply feeding the images we want to ourselves via self-talk and affirmations! Here's how it works: (Have a pencil and pen handy.)

a) Think about the type of person you want to become. Create an image of that person in your mind. See your ideal self.

b) Write a few short sentences using powerful adjectives to describe you in your finished state (i.e., strong, dependable, focused, committed, determined, confident, action-oriented).

c) Write your self-talk. Start each sentence with "I AM." A typical self-talk sentence would read like this: I am strong and determined in the pursuit of my goals. I am a positive and happy person, who is liked and respected. I am a winner. I always have the proper response to challenges.

d) Find a quiet room to sit and reaffirm the positives of yourself. Repeat your self-talk affirmations five to twenty times each day.

e) Repeat each affirmation with enthusiasm and excitement.

f) As you say your affirmations, see yourself in possession of the traits you're talking about. Keep telling yourself who you are, and in time you believe it and become that person!

2) **Visualization Exercises:** The second exercise involves using your creative imagination to visualize

your success. Visualization is a process that allows you to imagine yourself acting and responding to situations in a manner that helps you achieve the greatest results.

★ See yourself winning an award for academic excellence. See yourself handling difficult situations with ease or accomplishing anything YOU desire. See the picture of yourself (just as if you were watching a movie on a screen) and notice how you look, what you are feeling, who's at the event, and where the event is being held. Notice every detail. Hold your image for about fifteen to thirty seconds. Repeat the image or visualize another one.

★ Next, view the activities from inside yourself (like you normally would, from your eyes, looking out!). Look at the people and things around you. How are people responding to you? How are they looking? Repeat this exercise for about fifteen to thirty seconds as well. (Special Tip: Remember to add your emotions—during the visualization you should be excited and happy!)

For example, let's say you have to make a difficult presentation for the executive staff of your office. Visualize how you want this event to unfold. See yourself relaxed and calm as you make a great presentation!

Look outside yourself and notice the audience responding favorably to you. (Step-by-step instructions for this process are provided later in this chapter.)

Seeing the Self Succeed!

Many people don't achieve greatness because they cannot see themselves doing great things. The overwhelming majority of us see ourselves as very limited. Most of us begin early in life having high self-esteem, motivation, and creativity. As we get older, we begin to lose faith in our abilities. We stop dreaming to pursue more "practical" interests. At times, many of us have fantastic ideas for a business or product, but we never act on these ideas because we don't trust our own creativity. We don't see ourselves as special. We just don't think good things will happen to us, and we lose potentially great opportunities.

Why do we do this? Perhaps this is due to low self-esteem. Why do we often feel that only other people have what it takes to win? Many answers can be found within our own self-image because it was (and is) influenced by those who live with and around us. Take inventory of yourself; do you see yourself as worthy and capable of obtaining success? If not, this is most likely due to the limitations placed in your mind by others when you were very young.

All of us, when we are very young, are subjected to the thoughts, values, and beliefs of those who raise and nurture us. Many of those beliefs and values have

15

beneficial qualities that can be useful for these exciting times. However, some ideas and beliefs may not be pertinent for you at this time. Study and observe people around you. Can you determine who has limiting beliefs? Can you identify yours? Take a few moments to think about it. Have there ever been times when you quit *before* trying? Have you ever felt outclassed?

Get rid of limiting thoughts now! Every person on this earth is blessed with special talents and abilities in one or more areas. Each of us has the potential to do great things. It's important to remember that the most successful and famous people had to work very hard to achieve success. In short, successful people were once just like the rest of us. The only difference between them and us is their commitment to take actions necessary to make their dreams, their vision, a reality!

Don't internalize the limitations and pessimism of others. Develop a new vision triggered by a positive self-image, one that is energetic, highly charged, competent, courageous, and successful. Use your self-talk, to continually remind yourself of your own goodness!

Create Your New Vision

You can get everything you want in life, but you must determine what YOU want your future to hold, and place that vision in your mind. Now you are prepared to take the first step toward achieving your success. Start developing your vision today. Here are a few simple exercises that will help you. Begin doing these exercises for five to ten minutes daily. Use these exercises to enhance the ones described earlier in this chapter.

1) To be a winner, see yourself winning all of your day-to-day battles. Imagine a familiar problem or situation you face regularly. See yourself addressing the situation in a calm manner, with you ultimately winning.

2) Continue to develop a winning image and vision for yourself. Now is the time to look at your immediate and long-range visions. Write or draw a picture of yourself as you are now. Turn the paper over and write words that describe you (or draw yourself) as you would like to see yourself—at your best! What is the difference between your description and how you are now? Remember to see yourself in possession of all that you really want.

3) Be specific. Provide details about the kind of person you will be, your friends, the kind of car you'll drive, the house or apartment you'll live in, the money you will make on a weekly or monthly basis, if you are a student the grades you will achieve, etc.

4) Continue to refer to your written or drawn statements daily. Always keep your ultimate vision of success in your mind!

17

5) Affirm who you are with positive self-talk using "I am" statements (i.e., I am a doer. I am a person of action. I am confident, competent, and can handle any task).

This visualization principle has been discussed and tested at length by those who study the success phenomenon. It is a key ingredient for all who wish to be high achievers. This principle is very simple, but it works! Once you have established a vision of your success, and believe yourself to be worthy and capable of achieving it, YOU WILL HAVE IT.

Zig Zigler uses the analogy of our self-image as a constant, running movie within our minds. We have the power to change the image of our character, and we should, because our own image is often based on erroneous information. Dr. Maxwell Maltz, author of *The Magic Of Self Image Psychology*, suggests we can use our minds and imagination to rehearse how we want to act or win in difficult situations. As we allow these pictures of ourselves to become stronger, our actions follow. Do this at work or during your next sales call or meeting.

Expectations Come True!

Understand that no one else can make a vision for you. It can only be done for you, by you. If you don't expect much from life, you won't get much. If you believe you have the right talent to reach the next level, you will. A person with high expectations has lofty dreams and visions of great accomplishments. It's these strong visions that ultimately lead to a successful life.

Success is not an accident; it is obtained by those who have a definite vision that drives their thoughts and actions. Commit to developing a strong vision for yourself. **Start today.**

Control Your Mind to Obtain Your Power!!

●●●●●●●●●●

A s I begin this chapter, it's difficult to contain the excitement I feel for you. Controlling your mind is the second step toward the attainment of your success and the MOST IMPORTANT step in the creation of your success foundation. I feel this way because:

> The mind is the most powerful force known to man. It was given to us by our Spiritual Father (our power source) for the attainment of our dreams!!

Everything that IS, WAS, or WILL BE was, at one time, nothing more than a THOUGHT that was acted upon. EVERYTHING, including the:

★ car you drive
★ TV you watch

★ telephone you talk on
★ radio you listen to
★ video you watch
★ book you are reading now

...were *all* at one time nothing more than a THOUGHT, an idea that was acted upon!

This chapter will introduce techniques that will teach you how to use the power of your mind to get the things you want from life. This is a powerful opportunity for you, so let's get started!!

Let's make this clear: You will achieve the fruits of life (i.e., prosperity, good health, and happiness) when you learn to master the use of your most valuable resource—YOUR MIND! The good news is that only you can control your mind. *You* must plant the seeds of prosperity in your mind if you want your mind to help you achieve it. By practicing the exercises in this chapter, you can teach yourself how to focus your mind for greatness!

Why the Mind Is So Important

Before you can attain the things you want from life, you must be able to visualize them in your mind and believe you will have them (recall our last chapter). The Bible says it best in Mark 9:23—"If thou canst believe, all things are possible to him that believeth!" This verse describes the key concept of our theory:

1) The mind works to provide for you the things you *believe* you can have.

2) Most motivational speakers and success experts agree that the mind provides each of us with access to a tremendous power!

3) The mind acts like a magnet that draws to us the things we focus our thoughts upon, and those things we believe we deserve to have.

In spite of these fantastic truths, the overwhelming majority of Americans don't believe in their capacity to have whatever they desire. Many Americans suffer from low self-esteem (for any number of reasons) and have painted themselves into a safe, comfortable, and low-risk corner. This isn't a terrible life. However, there are a number of limitations to this kind of existence, including:

★ Struggling to make ends meet
★ Having little control over circumstances affecting you and your family
★ Working long and hard, leaving little time for inter-personal growth, family, and friendships
★ Lacking necessary funds for special activities
★ Having little money for sufficient savings—for college, retirement or disability
★ Suffering illness or accident that could take what little you manage to save

It doesn't have to be this way.

You are and always will be what you think you are! If you *believe* that you will become prosperous and successful, you will! For example, some people believe that they are destined to be sick. Their thoughts and fears of sickness fill them with stress and anxiety. Eventually, these people get ill. Why? Often the illness stems from the stress in their system caused by worry. The question is this: Is the person really ill, or did his mind simply give him what his thoughts focused on? The Bible says in Proverbs, chapter 23, verse 7, "As a man thinketh in his heart, so is he." People can only rise as high as their thoughts.

Here's a story that will illustrate this point. One day I was speaking to a junior high school counselor about **Success Training**. At the end of our conversation I asked the young counselor how she was doing, and if she was ready for another exciting school year. The counselor looked at me, gave me a sad smile, and shook her head "no." She explained to me that she was really hoping to find another opportunity at the local community college. She went on to explain that the only position available was an executive director's position. I said, "Great, go for it!" But this wasn't what the counselor wanted. Even though she met the minimum requirements for the job, she was afraid to apply for the position. She gave a number of reasons to justify her feelings: limited work experience, unwanted resentment from staff members with more years of experience, increased stress, etc. My question to you is this—what's wrong with this picture?

The problem, and the answers, lie in our thoughts! Most people have this type of conversation with themselves. They tell themselves why they CAN'T achieve a goal, or why they're afraid to try! The counselor gave many reasons for saying no to the position (even though she was unhappy in her current job). However, it was clear to me that her thoughts (and self-talk) did not empower her with the confidence needed to go after the goal. The counselor had the education and experience needed to qualify for the job, but she did not believe in her capacity to make the opportunity work. She focused on why she could not, or did not want the job! She focused on her own fears and (self-inflicted) limitations. Thus, she never pushed herself into actions needed to secure what could've been an exciting opportunity!

Anyone who truly wants a successful life should focus on the benefits of a desired goal or objective: What good would happen if you took that position, got the raise, and prepared yourself for success. *If you want to have success, your belief in yourself must be strong with no expected limitations!*

Keep your mind focused on prosperity, goodwill, good health, and strong and loving relationships. If you believe you are blessed and destined to win, then you will!

Believing Works!!

A common trait of highly successful people is a strong belief system. Successful and productive people believe in their abilities, their causes, and in great outcomes! *Winners always expect to find a way to win.* It is this strong belief system that sustains positive thinkers through the rough times, and continues to motivate them for challenging and rewarding opportunities.

Oprah Winfrey once said in an interview that she always believed she was destined for greatness. It was this belief that carried her to the top. Can your current belief system take you to the top?

How does one develop a winning belief system? By thinking positive thoughts, using prayer, self-talk, imagination, affirmation, and a strong belief in one's calling! Here are six easy steps for developing a success mentality!

1) *Develop A Strong Belief System.* Do you know what you really believe in? The one trait found in high achievers is a belief in their ability to make something great happen. To achieve success, you must believe strongly that you have the capacity to attain it and that you deserve it. The first step toward controlling your mind is deciding which direction your life will go. If you believe there's

power available to you through the use of your mind, then you've taken the first step toward making miracles happen. You can accomplish anything that you believe you can do!

2) *You Must Know What You Want.* The mind will help bring what you want to you, but it must know exactly what you want. If you are unsure of your goal or objective, think about your purpose or mission in life (remember chapter 1?). Here are some questions you should try:

★ What do I value most in life?
★ What have I done that provided me with the greatest sense of satisfaction and accomplishment?
★ What are my strengths?
★ What is my purpose?
★ What is it that I really want, e.g., love, health, prosperity, friends?

Take a few moments each night to think about these important questions. Have a pen and paper handy to record your answers. In a short time, you will have identified your mission and what you want to achieve in life. Now you're in business.

3) *Visualization.* This is one of the most powerful functions of the mind that can be controlled by you

to yield the results you desire. Again, take five to ten minutes each day to visualize your success. Read or state your goal(s) aloud. Close your eyes and run a moving picture of you achieving the goal (chapter 2).

4) *Affirm Yourself As a Winner.* It's what you say to yourself that counts. We are constantly talking to ourselves. What we say to ourselves directly affects our ability to achieve. The counselor in the earlier example probably told herself repeatedly, "I'm not good enough." Turn the negative into a positive. Each day, remind yourself of your strengths and successes that will strengthen your resolve and prepare you to win. Refer to chapter 2 for examples.

5) *Control Your Mind.* Keep your thoughts focused on the things you really want to happen. Watch as miracles begin to happen for you. Think it, talk it, see it, feel it—whatever you truly desire—and it's yours.

6) *Stay Positive.* Positive thoughts and high expectations activate your power source! As you control your mind/thoughts, continue substituting negative, defeatist thoughts with positive, uplifting ones. Keep your mind positive through the use of affirmations. These thoughts stimulate your creativity and energy. Positive thoughts strengthen our faith and resolve to achieve.

Why You Have Power

Substituting positve, productive, "can do" thoughts for negative ones is how your mind works to give you power.

I mentioned earlier that your mind is the most powerful tool known to man. I call the mind our power activator, because it is through our minds that we have a connection with a tremendous power source, our Spiritual Father. Most authors of success literature recognize a larger, more powerful life force in the universe. Some call this power "Super Conscience, Infinite Intelligence, Universal Sub-Conscience, The Oversoul, etc." Throughout this book, I refer to this great power as GOD.

What is exciting about this concept is the fact that we are all connected to this great power, through our minds! It is with the mind that we pray. We have access to the great power via meditation and prayer. As we strengthen and solidify this connection, we gain the POWER and guidance needed to obtain any goal. The power is activated into action by our command and grows in strength as our believing grows. Here's how it works:

> Ephesians 2:8—"For by grace are ye saved through faith; and not of yourselves: it is the gift of God."

> Mark 9:23—"If thou canst believe, all things are possible to him that believeth."

Mark 11:23, 24—"For verily I say unto you, that whosoever shall say unto this mountain, be thou removed, and be thou cast into the sea; and shall not doubt in his heart, but shall believe that those things which he saith shall come to pass; he shall have whatsoever he saith. Therefore I say unto you, what things soever ye desire, when ye pray, believe that ye receive them and ye shall have them."

Ephesians 3:19, 20—"And to know the love of Christ which passeth knowledge, that ye might be filled with all the fullness of God. Now unto Him that is able to do exceeding abundantly above all that we ask or think according to the POWER that worketh in us!"

These are powerful words written in support of my contention that the greatest power in the universe is at your disposal. This should excite you to no end, because the power resides in us, to be used by us!

YOU ARE A CHILD OF GOD; thus, you have POWER! Nothing should excite you more than to know that there is a great power in the universe willing and able to help you achieve everything you could possibly want in life. There is no fear within you. There are no limits to your potential.

Putting Your Power Source to Work for You!

Now that you know that your mind is your spiritual connection, it's time to put your power to work for your success. The power can and will work for you. Once you have turned on your omnipotent power source, you will find yourself filled with excitement and enthusiasm. You'll find it hard to contain yourself, and you will want to begin working on your goals immediately. You are CHARGED! As you think, meditate, and pray about a problem or opportunity, the answers that will come to you will be clear and precise and easy to understand. In fact, the solutions to many of your questions will seem so obvious that you'll wonder, "Was it always this simple?" Here are three steps to igniting your power source:

1) Identify what you want to achieve or accomplish. Remember, be specific.

2) Control your mind and focus your thoughts on your success goals. Write down your goals and spend time thinking about them. Find a quiet place where you can focus and concentrate daily on your objective. Keep a pen and piece of paper with you and record the answers or action steps that come to you. Try to spend five to ten minutes each day thinking. (NOTE: Don't strain! Relax and let the thoughts come easily to you. If nothing happens for the first few minutes don't become discouraged. Just reaffirm yourself and stay positive. In time, it will happen.)

3) Have faith. Believe strongly that you are worthy of your goals and that you will have them. Act as if they are already yours.

Remember, the Bible says you have power. This power works through your mind ignited by believing. If you do not or cannot control what and how you think, you have no power. As you focus your thoughts with faith, remember that *the stronger your belief system, the greater your power*. If you believe in yourself strongly enough, nothing can stop you. BELIEVE IT!

One last, very important note: As a child of God, your strength lies in love and goodness! Continue to believe in your goodness.

Note:

★ Keep this chapter in mind. It plays a critical role in goal achievement. Your focused thoughts, and desires will bring your goal(s) to you.

Stay Positive

This is a very exciting time for you! You're already starting to think about things in a different way. You're beginning to see the type of positive and fulfilling life you want to build for yourself, and you're thinking about action steps you'll take to make it happen! To keep your momentum going, *Stay Positive!* Continue to think positively about your chances for success.

Throughout history, too many people with talent, intelligence, ideas, and vision fell short of their goals simply because they experienced setbacks. Many have tried to achieve their dreams, yet after a few failures, most quit or resigned themselves to the notion that their idea or dream was not attainable. These people lost their momentum. They didn't keep their thoughts positive.

You are spiritually grounded in goodness, and this goodness provides you with the power needed to achieve your dreams! You deserve success and will have it if you are positive in your beliefs. Clear your mind of all fear, worry, anxiety, doubt, hatred, and guilt, and prepare yourself for the many great opportunities that are coming your way!

Nothing worthwhile is ever easy. If being successful was easy, everyone would be successful! During your success journey, you will experience setbacks, disappointments, and defeats. How you respond to these unpleasant situations determines the strength of your faith and how committed you are to achieving your goals. Train yourself to always look for opportunities with every setback. Here are five effective strategies for keeping your positive momentum:

1) Remember your vision and how you plan to attain it. Use self-talk.

2) Remember your spiritual connection. You are a child of God and you're grounded in goodness!

3) Within every setback lie opportunities.

4) You have control. You control your mind, thoughts, and actions!

5) You are never defeated until your mind accepts defeat.

AND . . . expect to win!

Strength through a Positive Attitude!

If you truly want to be a success, you must develop and maintain a positive attitude. If you are mentally positive, your ability to influence others increases, thus increasing your opportunity to create business relationships and friendships that may profit you down the road.

When you develop a positive attitude, you become happier and more self-confident. It will help you overcome hardships. Most important, it allows you to believe that whatever the situation, YOU will ultimately end up on top! Troubles at work? No problem; begin immediately looking for the opportunities that are borne out of difficulties.

A perfect example of a person with a positive attitude is Carter Godwin Woodson, (1875–1950). Carter Godwin Woodson:

★ Was born in 1875 to a poor family of Black tenant farmers.
★ Because of family farming commitments, never received formal education until he was twenty-one years old.
★ Received his bachelor of arts degree from the University of Chicago.
★ Went to Paris to study at the Sorbonne.
★ Received his Ph.D. from Harvard.
★ Authored *The Mis-Education Of The Negro* in 1933.
★ Became the founder of Negro History Week (which is now Black History Month).

Dr. Woodson was born in a poor Black family and lived in an oppressive environment just a few short years after the end of the Civil War and the emancipation of the slaves. (Can you imagine how tough that must have been for him?) Yet his personal initiative, drive, and determination to succeed were BIGGER than the obstacles in his way! Dr. Woodson had to maintain a positive attitude to keep his eyes on his dream while he waited twenty-one years to be able to attend school! Dr. Woodson was focused. He had high standards and was determined to live his life as he chose to live it. He had a strong and positive belief in his abilities, and he went out into the world and made great things happen!

Develop and Maintain a Positive Attitude

To win and win consistently, develop and maintain a positive attitude that will help you stay up when the world tries to knock you down. Here are five strategies for creating a positive attitude:

1) *There will always be a positive for every negative you encounter.* There is something positive in every experience. When you meet with defeat and setbacks, stay optimistic because something better will come soon. When defeat comes, just say, "This means there's something better heading my way!"

2) *See Challenges as Opportunities!* Each time you are challenged, be grateful. The challenge provides you with another opportunity to display your

talents, determination, and faith. Each day say to yourself, "Challenges bring out the best in me!"

3) *Never Beaten.* You are never, ever defeated until YOU tell yourself that you are defeated! You are never defeated until your mind admits defeat! Staying positive means that whatever the particular situation, you always expect to end up on top!

4) *Give thanks daily* for your blessings. Remember your spiritual connection.

5) *Say—"That's Good!"* In their book *Success Through a Positive Mental Attitude*, Napoleon Hill and Clement Stone point out that no situation is ever bad unless you truly believe it to be. By saying, "That's good," your mind automatically begins to focus on the positive!

Continue to tell yourself that you are a positive person. You have strength due to a strong belief system. Thus, you expect to win in every situation. When faced with adversity, look for its hidden blessings. You will win in the end if you truly believe that you will.

Moving Forward with Action

● ● ● ● ● ● ● ● ●

Now you're beginning to understand the difference between those who are winners in life and those who aren't. You're beginning to see how a person can be limited or empowered by his or her own self-image and beliefs. You know that one is limited only to the extent one accepts self-imposed limitations. Your mind is working and you are beginning to recognize your power.

You're learning how to build a successful life. By now you should know how to:

1) Appreciate and feel good about yourself.

2) Create a positive and exciting vision of your future.

3) Control your mind with ideas by focusing positively and expectantly on what you really want.

Now...IT'S TIME TO GET INTO ACTION!! The Bible says, "Faith without works is dead." You've taken time to visualize the way you'd like your life to be. However, you will never attain your goals until you start making things happen! You cannot achieve your desired objective(s) through thought alone! You must get out there, test your ideas, and put your plans into ACTION!

Action: The Ultimate Test of Your Faith

Throughout history, many people have had great thoughts and ideas that they ultimately took to the grave with them because they never put their ideas into action. All of us are blessed with creative talent(s) and the ability to think! Yet ideas, no matter how great, mean little if no one acts on them. Lack of ACTION is the main reason so many of us never realize our dreams.

The ultimate test of your faith lies in action. If you truly believe you can be successful in a certain area, what's stopping you from having that success? If you believe you are destined to do great things, get into action and begin making things happen—NOW!

An example of a man of action is Abraham of the Bible. God promised to make Abraham the father of a great nation, and that he would be blessed with a son, who would be named Isaac. This doesn't seem outrageous, except that Abraham was ninety-nine years old when God made him this offer! Even Abraham's wife,

40

Sarah, was ninety years old. The Bible discusses Abraham in Romans 4:19-22:

> And being not weak in faith, he considered not his own body now dead, when he was about one hundred years old, neither yet the deadness of Sarah's womb: So he staggered not at the promise of God through unbelief; but was strong in faith giving glory to God; And being fully persuaded that, what He had promised, he was able also to perform. And therefore it was imputed to him for righteousness. *[Emphasis mine.]*

You see, Abraham ACTED on the promise of God. Because his belief in God was strong, he went into action to create the results he knew were his (his son Isaac)! The twelve tribes of Israel owed their very existence to Abraham's faith.

Just like Abraham, if you have an idea, a strong belief in your abilities, and a plan of action, ACT on it and your actions will be fruitful! You'll be surprised at how things will seem to fall into place for you once you begin taking action!

Nothing to Lose, Everything to Gain

The great thing about taking action is that you can't lose! When you act, two things are bound to happen:

1) You'll get what you want and/or need to make your dreams a reality, or

41

2) You won't get what you want, but you will learn what adjustments are needed to make your dreams a reality.

Either way, YOU WIN! The only way you ever lose is when you fail to act!

You have nothing to fear. Action defeats fear! When you take action, only good things can happen to you. Either you get it or you learn from your mistakes what is needed to get it. Fear leads to inactivity. If you fail to act on your plans or ideas, eventually someone else will! Here's a perfect example of what can happen when you are afraid to act.

Walter Hunt, born 1796, was considered a genius. He was given credit for inventing the fountain pen, sewing machine, burglar and fire alarms, and the breech-loading, cartridge-firing rifle. Yet, Hunt died practically unknown and in poverty. There were many factors that contributed to his situation, but let's look at a couple of things that went wrong:

★ The lockstitch sewing machine, designed in 1834, was never promoted by Hunt. He feared that the machine would put thousands of seamstresses out of work. Years later these same sewing machines were sold commercially.

★ The breech-loading, cartridge-firing rifle, though invented by Hunt, bears the name of the man who marketed it—Winchester.

Walter Hunt was a brilliant man, yet he died poor because he lacked the courage and faith needed to properly promote his ideas and inventions.

To have success, convince yourself that you are a person of action. Believe in your ideas and act on them! If you don't, someone else will.

Action Kills Procrastination

Procrastination is the killer of achievement. As I mentioned earlier, many people will get a fantastic idea that could get them on their way to a happy and prosperous life, yet procrastinate until the idea or opportunity to act is lost.

Winners seldom procrastinate. They are people of action. Action kills procrastination! Here are five ways to overcome procrastination:

1) Schedule important events and actions that must be taken for your success.

2) There is never a more perfect time than the present. Do you really think that there will ever be a more perfect time? Develop a strong sense of urgency. Get used to acting on issues quickly! Do it now!

3) Develop an action plan. Break down your plan into manageable steps. Determine the time needed to achieve each step, then plan and schedule these activities accordingly.

43

4) Remind yourself of the benefits that come from action and the results you want! Stay focused on your goal!

5) Reward yourself for taking action.

Action = Success!

In order for you to have the things you want in life, you must take action to make things happen. This means that you are in total control of your life. Here are some strategies for getting and staying actively in pursuit of your goals. Good luck!

1) Each night, write out an "Action Checklist" describing one to three action steps you will take the next day. These actions should be determined by your goals and priorities, and what will yield your desired outcomes.

2) Make sure that no matter how busy your day, you complete a task that will move you closer to your identified goal or objective. Remember your "Action Checklist."

3) Use your spiritual connection daily for guidance, then ACT on your ideas.

4) Make a note of each obstacle you successfully hurdle and note every defeat or setback you

experience (there's learning in both experiences). Remember to keep your eyes open for new opportunities with every setback.

5) When in doubt, ACT! Doing something may stimulate your creativity or open other avenues that may prove beneficial to you.

6) Use your power and faith in God. Believe that your efforts will be successful and you'll be amazed at how far you can go! Expect to WIN!

Get Going!

How Bad Do You Want It?

PERSEVERANCE, COMMITMENT, AND DETERMINATION

What separates the winners from others? Were you to ask people if they'd like to be prosperous and successful, the overwhelming majority would respond with a resounding YES! Yet while most of us say we want to be successful, only a few achieve our definition of "success."

There is nothing easy about achieving worthwhile goals and objectives. This is why you must look in the mirror each day and ask yourself three simple questions:

1) Do I know what I want (what's my definition of success)?

2) Do I deserve to have it?

3) Am I willing to do what it takes to have it?

You now possess all the tools you will ever need to make good things happen. Remember what we've discussed thus far:

★ *Visualization*—See yourself as a winner, worthy of success. See yourself having successes. Create your future, create an exciting vision!

★ *Control Your Mind*—Focus your mental energies on your dreams using your spiritual connection to guide and empower you toward your identified objectives.

★ *Staying Positive*—The best way to deal with life's disappointments is by staying positive. Expect to eventually end up on top. Learn from setbacks.

★ *Moving to Action*—Take the ideas and plans you were thinking about and get into action. There's no winning without action.

If you internalize these time-tested success strategies into your habit patterns, you will immediately begin to notice how much your ability to produce will improve. Your life will change because your thoughts, expectations, and actions have changed! You are now prepared to win because you expect to win!

The most exciting aspect regarding this whole can-do, success mentality is that once you develop this aspect of yourself, YOU become virtually unstoppable! Keep your mind focused on your goals, be faithful, use your affirmations, stay positive, and in a short time *you will be unstoppable!*

48

Now you must see your projects, goals, and aspirations through to completion. To ensure your success, you must immediately begin to build a layer of toughness, determination, and commitment into your character. You must persevere through difficult times. You can always win as long as you are determined and persistent enough to do so.

Determination and Perseverance Is the Key

Now you're on your way. You are positive and making things happen. Each day you're telling yourself, "I am unstoppable!" Does this mean that everything is going to work out perfectly for you from now on? Not likely. You will continue to have setbacks and disappointments. You will continue to have defeats and sometimes just plain bad luck. It's safe to say it may even get tougher, the closer you get to obtaining your ultimate goals!

It's important to remember that success and failure go hand in hand. How can you ever achieve anything worthwhile if there are no risks? Most of the people who fail are those attempting to make something great happen! You will always be average if you never try to reach for what is above average! Even millionaires meet with failure. The average American millionaire goes bankrupt 3.5 times! The reasons so many of these millionaires still achieve success is due to their perseverance and determination to WIN! They were never defeated in their minds!

All truly successful people have failed! This is why you must discipline yourself to prepare for the

49

challenges ahead. The first hurdle you will need to conquer is the fear of failure. *All great people have experienced failure. However, it's not failure that breaks men—it's their reaction to failure that determines who ultimately wins!* WINNERS are never truly beaten. To these, defeat/failure is only a temporary setback. Here's a short list of just a few great individuals who have experienced failure:

ISIAH THOMAS

FAILED: Threw a bad pass with only seconds remaining; cost Detroit Pistons a conference championship.

WON: Came back two years later as team's MVP to win back-to-back world championships.

MALCOLM X

FAILED: Spent years in prison for robbing and stealing.

WON: Became chief spokesman for Nation of Islam and renowned leader of African Americans.

NELSON MANDELA

FAILED: Spent more than twenty years in a South African prison.

WON: Became president of South Africa.

"COLONEL" HARLAN SANDERS

FAILED: Turned down by over a thousand restaurant owners who were not interested in his chicken recipe.

WON: Stuck with his idea and died a wealthy man with thousands of Kentucky Fried Chicken restaurants throughout the world.

WALT DISNEY

FAILED: Went bankrupt and was hospitalized after suffering a nervous breakdown.

WON: Died a tremendously wealthy man after building the Disney empire.

DON KING

FAILED: Served years in prison for manslaughter.

WON: Now a multimillion-dollar boxing promoter and most influential man in the sport.

The trait that separates great people from the mediocre is that the great ones RARELY ACCEPT DEFEAT. For winners, failure only strengthens their resolve and determination to continue until their goal is ultimately obtained. They are committed and determined to never quit. Winners persevere!

Remain Committed

To achieve success, we often must leave our comfort zones. You will experience the unknown and try things most people wouldn't have the courage to try. Success requires some risk, which can lead to disappointments. Without risk, there is no reward. Expect setbacks, welcome them, and view defeat as a learning tool that will ultimately serve to benefit you in some way.

Those who have ever won at anything first committed themselves to winning. This is why you must continue to live your life with zest, excitement, and determination! Commit yourself to winning. Tell yourself daily that nothing can stop you and that you will persist until you have all that you so richly deserve. Your persistence and determination demonstrate your faith and commitment to succeed.

Perseverance breaks down barriers that stand in the way of your success. YOU WILL HAVE IT. Remember the words of former President Calvin Coolidge:

> Nothing in the world can replace persistence. Talent will not; nothing is more common than unsuccessful men with talent. Genius will not; unregarded genius is almost a proverb. Education will not; the world is full of educated derelicts. Persistence and determination alone are omnipotent!

Getting What You Want

THE MAGIC OF GOAL SETTING!

The first time I tried to use and perfect the success strategies discussed in this book, I didn't understand why it was necessary to visualize the things I wanted to happen. I thought a person could achieve success just by having a general idea about what he wanted from life. This is probably the reason I was unsuccessful in achieving success in my life until now. Like many of you:

1) I didn't know what I really wanted.

2) I didn't know how to use the power of my mind.

3) I didn't understand the magic of goal setting.

You must know what you want and you must focus your mental powers on your dreams and desires. This is the reason goal setting is a critical exercise for all who wish to have success. Goals help us to stay focused. Goals allow us to direct our energies by clarifying and crystallizing the things we want to accomplish. Once we are certain that we know what we really want, the action steps we'll take to attain our dreams become clearer.

Many studies have determined that goal setting is a trait consistently found in high achievers, yet only a few people bother doing it (only about 3 percent of the population). Ask several people if they have identified their life's goals. If so, ask whether any of them have written their goals down. Finally, ask yourself how many of these people would you consider to be successful?

Goals are our written plans for success. They can and will work for you! There is not a personal success professional today who doesn't appreciate the power and effectiveness of goal setting! Goals provide the direction needed for success.

Most experts on personal success agree that we have a tremendous potential to achieve through the use of our power source, our minds (spiritual connection). However, this power is useless if it has no clear objective or target to focus upon. If we don't focus our mental energies, then our power is wasted on frivolous and trivial matters. Goals provide the target, the direction needed for our thoughts, energies, and activities.

Most Don't Do It!

Most people don't set clear life goals. Less than 4 percent of America's population have identified goals and committed them to paper. There are many reasons why most people don't take the time to set goals. Many fail to set goals because they don't know how to do it. Others don't set them because they're afraid of being ridiculed if they are unsuccessful in achieving their goals. Some people will try to set goals but quickly give up on them at the first hint of failure. The rest are just plain lazy! However, of those Americans who write out their life's goals, the great majority are successful in reaching them.

Steps to Goal Setting: Start Today!!

Enough talk; let's get started. As you begin this process it's important for you to remember that the attainment of your goals requires you to have a strong desire to achieve your objective. There should be a definite reason for the attainment of the goal. This purpose will serve to motivate, energize, and ignite your creative capacity.

Secondly, you must BELIEVE that you deserve to have your goals. To achieve them, you must believe in your abilities to succeed and control your own destiny. Expect to win! This is the most exciting aspect of life. Here are some characteristics of high quality goals:

> **Specific**—You must pinpoint exactly what you want. Concentrate on two or three primary goals for each area of your life. Balance between short-term, immediate, and long-term goals.

Believable—See yourself in possession of the goal. If you can't see it, you don't believe it. If you don't believe it, you can't achieve it!

Personal—Only you can make goals for yourself. Only you know what you truly want. Don't set goals based on the interests and desires of others. If it doesn't benefit you in some way, you will quickly lose the desire to achieve it.

Positive—Achieving the goal should have a reward value. The goal should benefit you, or enhance your life in some manner. In fact, the more benefits you can list, the greater your desire and ability to manifest the goal.

Challenging—Goals should provide a challenge. They should stimulate you to be your best. They should cause you to take risks. This is how you make progress in life. Winners truly enjoy a challenge!

Time Specific—Each goal should have an allotted time period or target date for its attainment.

Balanced—Goals should address each aspect of your life:

★ *Relationship/Social*—Are the people in your life (family, friends, etc.) energy givers, or do they drain you of energy and enthusiasm? Surround yourself with doers and go-getters.

★ *Educational*—Always be prepared for learning opportunities. Be sharp! Look for ways to improve your life, expand your mind, and prepare yourself for success.

★ *Career/Financial*—What do you ultimately see yourself doing to make a living? What type of income would you like to have? When do you want to have it attained? How much money do you want to save? How much will you need for a comfortable retirement?

★ *Physical Fitness*—Keep yourself in shape. Work out at least three times a week. Set a workout schedule and follow it. Build yourself so you will have the energy needed to succeed.

★ *Spiritual*—Your power source. Feed it every day. Love it and it loves you even more! You are a child of God. Maintain and strengthen your connection.

Written—Your goals should be plainly stated and written down on paper. The goals should be reviewed several times a week. Use 3 x 5 cards for daily review.

Changeable—Your goals will always change and evolve as you grow and succeed. While you achieve one goal your thoughts will turn to the next (more challenging) goal.

With all this in mind, here are steps in the magic of goal setting! Use these ideas as listed or modify to your comfort. What's important is that you take the time to decide your plan of action:

1) At the top of a sheet of paper write, "What I Really Want!" Without thinking about it too much, begin writing down whatever you think you want. Don't worry about the price or how outrageous your desire may be, simply write down whatever comes to mind. Stop writing when you feel all the important areas of your life have been addressed.

2) Identify the top ten items by numbering them from one to ten. Separate items into life categories listed earlier—i.e., interpersonal, spiritual, career/financial, etc. Don't worry if your answers aren't evenly divided by each category. Address the areas that concern you now!

3) Put each of your top goals on a separate sheet of paper. Write your goal statement on the top of the paper. On the left side margin write in one of four time periods to determine how long it will take to achieve them—1) one month, 2) six months, 3) one year, or 4) two years. Now you have identified

what you will accomplish and when it will be yours.

4) On the same sheet of paper, write the word "BEN-EFITS" in the left margin of the page. How does the accomplishment of this goal benefit you or your family? List all the benefits. This is the "why" part of your goal sheet.

5) Write two affirmations or self-talk statements for each of the top ten goals you identified.

6) List talents or skills you currently possess that will help you attain your goal. What can you do now to bring the goal closer? How can you utilize the skills you have now to your benefit? Next, list the people in your life that can offer assistance or possess resources to assist you.

7) On the same sheet of paper write "ACTION PLAN." Review your goals list and identify at least three action steps that you will take right away. Whats the first thing you need to do?

NOTE:

This is also a good time to take inventory of yourself. For example, what strengths or resources do you now possess that can help you attain your goal? In addition, ask yourself, what resources do I need to obtain (i.e., degrees, certification, or training), and what personal traits do I need to strengthen for the achievement of my goals? Identify what you need and get into action to make the necessary changes.

Additional Tips for Success

Another step that will help you stay focused on your goals is to write your goals on 3 x 5 cards. Keep the cards with you and review them during breaks and other slow times during your day. Each card should be written as a positive affirmation. Repeat the affirmation to yourself and then aloud (if possible). As you review your goal cards, visualize yourself in possession of the goal.

Finally, you should begin visualizing and imagining your life with your goals achieved! Again, think of your goals and see yourself with it. Now ask yourself, "What am I feeling?" Bring your emotions to full realization. Note them. Are you happy? Do you have a sense of pride and accomplishment? Do you feel excitement? Feel the emotions each time you think about your goals. Don't forget the emotional ties to all of your actions. Your goals should make you feel good inside.

Get ready for the realization of your dreams. Exciting things are going to happen!

Success Habits to Live By!

This is the most exciting time of your life! Doesn't it feel great to have total confidence in knowing that no matter what the circumstance, you will be all right!? I LOVE IT!!

The skills and strategies we've discussed so far provide you with all the confidence and strength needed to achieve your dreams for success! However, to maintain your momentum, begin now to develop habits that will enhance your chances for long-term success! Your actions tell others what you think of yourself! If you are truly a winner, you will show it in everything you do. To achieve any worthwhile goal requires the collaboration and/or the assistance of others. Your ability to work with others will greatly affect your ability to get positive things done for yourself and others. This chapter will help you in your dealings with a variety of life's challenges.

What are the habits we need to internalize in order to win with people? What disciplines do we need to adopt? How can we get people to like us and want to assist us? How do we convince those with the ability to hire and use resources for our cause, to help us? These are just a few of the exciting areas we will address in this chapter, so let's get started!

How to Develop Winning Habits

In addition to having the character traits of strong belief in self, focused thoughts, and goal setting, successful people also exhibit winning habits. These habits allow them to establish rapport with others, and make favorable first impressions by creating win/win opportunities for all. Successful, high achieving people have a way of getting others to like, respect, and trust them. People feel very comfortable in their company and desire to be around them.

The objective of this chapter is to teach you commonsense strategies for winning with people from peers and classmates to teachers, employers, and future business partners. These ideas are also useful for developing better relationships with family members and casual acquaintances. This chapter will help you become known as an individual of quality and personal excellence!

There are four major categories we will address:

★ Winning People Skills
★ School, Work, and Business

* Time Management
* Personal Excellence

Winning People Skills
(Getting People to Like You)

All of us need and want quality people to like us. Many of us, however, have no idea how to make people like us. Here are seven easy rules to remember for winning with people:

1) **SMILE**: Sounds simple, but always remember to smile at an individual when you are introduced to them or while walking up to meet them. Make eye contact, smile, and say, "Hello, my name is _____, very nice to meet you!" Make your eyes sparkle and smile warmly.

2) **REMEMBER NAMES**: Difficult, but doable! Upon hearing one's name, immediately begin saying it repeatedly in your mind. Say the name at every opportunity when speaking to that person. Reaffirm to yourself, "I remember names!"

3) **THINK GOOD THOUGHTS**: As you socialize with others, keep your mind filled with good thoughts. Each time someone stops to talk with you, think good thoughts about that person. Tell yourself that the person speaking is sincere, honest, competent, likable, interesting, and intelligent. We've talked a lot about the power of the mind. It's

63

amazing how the mind can send signals that can affect others.

Sometimes we can sense how a person really feels about us. If we try to think good thoughts about others, there's a good chance they will sense how you feel and respond to you positively, as well. Think positively about teachers and bosses, too. In a short time, you will have the admiration and respect of others. It really works!

4) **TAKE A SINCERE INTEREST IN OTHERS**: Listen to the stories others have to tell about themselves. Encourage people to talk about themselves, their interests, dreams, and aspirations. Ask questions. Speak of yourself only when encouraged to do so. Let the other person know you are interested in them and that you find them incredibly exciting. People love to talk about themselves and like people who find them interesting!

5) **SINCERELY PRAISE OTHERS**: There's good in everyone. Always find something good to say about people. If a person on your sales team works hard through difficult times, say something positive about his efforts in front of others. Watch as he lights up with pride. If a person is a sharp dresser and wears something nice to school or on the job, tell him/her how much you like the way he or she looks. The same can apply for haircuts, makeup, etc. People are

generally insecure and self-conscious. If you help them feel good about themselves, they will appreciate you all the more!

6) **DON'T BOTHER TO ARGUE:** Disagreements are a part of relationships today. There seldom is a time when two people can agree on every issue, so it's understandable when arguments and disagreements occur. Never argue! *Arguing is not an effective way of getting people to see things your way.* When was the last time you changed your opinion or idea after an argument? An argument doesn't help people listen to your point of view. The only thing an argument does is make people angry! No one ever wins an argument. It is absolutely useless to argue!

7) **STAY POSITIVE—SHOW ENTHUSIASM:** Always be positive and enthusiastic around others. When you meet someone, greet them with high expectations and enthusiasm. Make them feel warm and welcomed. Let them know to call on you if they ever have a problem or need assistance. Show people how to win, not whine! Keep a smile on your face and always expect things to work out. Be an energy giver. Be supportive of other's dreams and goals! You'll be amazed how people will gravitate toward you because you're always so positive and upbeat!

Stay at it. If a certain approach does not work for a person, or a situation, try a different approach. Keep testing responses until you get the outcomes you desire.

School, Work, and Business

Most people behave a certain way or respond to events in a certain manner because they've learned and practiced those responses. Each of us acts in ways that fit our own self-image, and as we continually practice these actions, they become habits. Each day we continue to develop habits that remain with us for the rest of our lives. Now is the time to develop quality habits that will benefit you on your success journey. Learn these responses early, practice them, internalize them, and they will provide a success blueprint for your educational and professional aspirations. Here are eight commonsense steps for success at school and/or work:

1) **BELIEVE IN YOURSELF:**
Before you can ever achieve in life, you must have a strong belief in your ability to succeed. Believe in your abilities to do whatever is required to succeed at any endeavor. If you want learning to become easier, first believe that you can learn! Think of your mind as a sponge that can retain all it hears and reads. If it's a particularly tough work assignment, believe that you have the capacity, energy, and intelligence necessary to succeed.

Just remember that you can do whatever you believe you can!

2) **WHAT IS REQUIRED?:**
What are the steps you need to take to meet your goals? Know what's expected and needed for success. What do you need to excel in your job? Learn what you need to do in any situation. Write down the steps needed, focus, then put your plan into action. Also discuss work expectations, goals and standards with your boss!

3) **BE PREPARED:**
Discipline yourself and prepare for every aspect of your class or job. Have you prepared yourself for success? Ask yourself, do I have all the necessary information available for a successful response? If your employer asks you to participate on a work team or task force, obtain knowledge on the subject you will work on. Always be prepared.

4) **BE ON TIME:**
There's nothing people hate more than to have to wait for someone. A person who is consistently late lacks respect and credibility with his peers, and will not endear himself with an employer. Being punctual shows that you value other people's time as well as your own. Make a commitment to be on time for all engagements. There is no secret to being on time; it's an attitude, a frame of mind. Once you decide in your mind to be on time, you will.

5) **WRITE IT DOWN:**

A mistake many of us make is overestimating our ability to remember. We think that once we hear it, we will remember it, if it's important enough. Unfortunately, most of us are not blessed with great memories. We tend to forget more than we like to admit. Whenever you're in a conference, class, or a meeting, write down the important issues discussed. Make a habit of always keeping a pen and paper handy and write it down! Information is power!

6) **DO IT NOW:**

This is one of the most important characteristics of successful people. When you are given a task or project, don't put it off until later. Do it now. Develop a sense of urgency within you, so that your mind constantly reminds you to do it now! This attitude defeats procrastination and increases your ability to get the results you want. *Your power lies in your ability to act.*

A person who can get things done early or on time is of great value in our society. You increase job security and promotional opportunities when you consistently demonstrate the ability to get things done in a timely manner. *Remember, you are an individual who loves action.* Keep that sense of urgency. When ideas hit you, when you're given assignments and projects, when someone makes a request for assistance, don't put it off—DO IT NOW!

7) **ENJOY THE EXPERIENCE:**
"This, too, shall pass." This simply means that nothing lasts forever. You won't be in school for long. You won't be working the job you're at for long (I hope you have plans for greater opportunities). Take the time to enjoy each experience you have. Have enthusiasm for everything you do. Take pride in your efforts and enjoy the challenge of being the best. Continue to affirm that you are living and enjoying yourself each moment. Enjoy each of life's challenges and always expect to end up on top. This makes life extremely exciting.

You can create excitement, so do it! School assignments become easier. Work is more enjoyable. Employers are more likely to hire a person with determination and enthusiasm than a person who lacks these qualities. Get together with a friend or two who are ambitious like yourself, and challenge them to see who can get the highest grades, the best jobs, etc. *No challenge is difficult when it's enjoyed and viewed with enthusiasm.* You will find that life is much more fun when you look at it as an exciting challenge. Enjoy yourself!

8) **FINANCIAL MANAGEMENT:**
Financial freedom will provide you with the resources you need to develop your plans and

ideas for excellence. The odds are good that YOU will soon have large sums of money. It's imperative that you learn to understand money and the relationship between time, inflation, and money!

Your first step is to learn about the many different investment and savings vehicles available to you. Establish investment goals and research which investment vehicles will provide the greatest opportunity for achieving your financial objectives.

Always try to save at least 10 percent of your gross income each month. There are a number of no-load mutual funds, many that will take as little as fifty dollars a month to start, that can provide you with an excellent return on your investment. Blue chip stocks and savings bonds are other options to be researched. It's important to develop the habit of saving now.

Saving and investing your money allows your savings to accrue interest, which helps offset the value-robbing characteristics of inflation. Over time, your money can grow to tremendous sums. Inflation shrinks the value of money. A good savings and investment plan allows your money to maintain its value.

Begin now by subscribing to investment publications, or go to your school or public library and review articles from *The Wall Street Journal*, *Money*, *Kiplinger's Personal Finance*, and *Mutual Fund Magazine*. You might also want to call your local investment professional at Merrill Lynch, Dean Witter, or personal banker to get investment ideas and additional information.

Time Management

It's good to be an individual of action! It's good to want to do it now! However, you must make sure you're doing those things that are the most important. If you want to be effective in your life, make certain you have prioritized your activities to accomplish those activities that will benefit you the most. This is a vital variable in your success equation. You always have time to do the important things! Here are some tips for developing good activity/time management habits:

1) IDENTIFY YOUR GOAL/OBJECTIVE: You must know what you want to accomplish in order to properly plan your steps for its achievement. Identify your goal. Plan your actions based upon what you really want.

2) DEVELOP AN ORGANIZATIONAL SYSTEM: Purchase a calendar or daily planning tool that will help you in organizing your activities. It should be something you can keep with you at all times. Your planning system should have the following basic components to help you manage your activities:

   a) a yearly calendar

   b) a monthly calendar

c) a daily calendar with time included

d) a phone listing

Use your tool to list, schedule, and prioritize all of your important events. A daily planner allows you to keep track of your activities, meetings, special dates, and engagements. In addition, a planner lets you identify and prioritize your most important events and projects, and follow their progress to the end. Finally, the tool is useful for taking notes of special meetings, etc., for quick and easy reference in recalling important discussions. Electronic data organizers are also very useful tools.

3) **MAKE "TO DO" LISTS**: "To do" lists are simple and effective ways of staying active and productive in the pursuit of your goals. Each evening, take 15 to 30 minutes think about the things you want and need to accomplish the next day. List these activities in your daily planner. The practice of making "to do" lists helps you stay active and focused on the things you want to accomplish.

4) **PRIORITIZE YOUR LIST**: Your next step is to prioritize your "to do's." There will be days when it will be almost impossible to do all that you would like. If you find yourself in a bind for time, prioritize your activities. Identify those items that must be done that day and put a check or a star by them. Make sure these items are given your utmost attention the next day.

Another method is to identify your top four to six items. Imagine that you only had time to do three of your most important items, which three would it be? Rank all of the items, then take your top three priorities and complete them during the day. There is also the simple ABC model for prioritization: A = actions you must do; B = actions you should do; and C = actions that would be good to do. Any of these prioritization methods ensures that you're getting the important projects and activities done.

5) **REPEAT:** Repeat the process of making a "to do" list and prioritize it each night. Make this practice a habit and you will always be productive. Use your planner to expand your efforts. List the goals you'd like to achieve for the next month and each month thereafter. Set priorities and watch as you achieve success after success.

Personal Excellence

There's something very special about you. People have begun to notice you more. You're already beginning to stand out in a crowd. You carry yourself like a winner. People are already saying good things about you. They see you are a person with a commitment to get the things you want from life. It's happening! You're becoming a winner right before everyone's eyes. Keep a strong sense of personal excellence as part of your character. Here's how you demonstrate Personal Excellence:

1) **COMMIT TO EXCELLENCE**: A person who thinks highly of himself will reflect that feeling in everything he does. His actions tell of his character. *Winners make a habit of always giving more than what is expected.* Martin Luther King Jr. always urged his followers to display personal excellence in their job duties, regardless of how menial the task. As a winner, take pride in your abilities to do work assignments, duties, tasks, and projects in an excellent manner. Always give more than what is expected and you will be given every opportunity to succeed. Develop a burning pride to be the best.

2) **SURROUND YOURSELF WITH EXCELLENCE**: As a person of excellence, you will meet many people who believe in the things you do. They will want to work with you and will assist you in your endeavors. As we discussed earlier, to achieve anything great requires the help of others. These are the people you should recognize and continually associate with. Surround yourself with people of excellence! Surround yourself with energy givers. These are people who are excited about their abilities to make good things happen. They are doers who rarely make excuses for failures in life. They are like you in

that they love action and will be supportive of activities that are above the norm.

People of excellence believe strongly in "GOING FOR IT!" Winners continue to win when they surround themselves with people who also are determined to win. Associate with people who are winners like yourself. Be good to them and reward them for their loyalty and assistance. Always remember those who help you along the way, and they'll continue to help you.

3) **GET INVOLVED**: You are an individual of class, character, and distinction. As a person of action, you should be actively involved in social organizations, sports, clubs, etc. Get involved and make things happen. Whenever you are at a social function, be gracious and express appreciation to your hosts for inviting you. Be gracious and friendly to all members of the host family.

4) **BE GOOD TO OTHERS—GIVE SOMETHING BACK**: People may forget the good things you do, but people will never forget how you treat them. If you want to be remembered as a person of quality, always be good to others. This shouldn't be difficult for you to do. You are a child of God. You are grounded in goodness and love. Your heart is full of love and kindness. This love is power that will help your success efforts. You

continue to practice winning people skills discussed earlier in this chapter. The final habit will bless you tenfold: Always give something back. Giving is so important to your success that I've written a whole chapter on it!

One of the reasons you will be blessed to have all you ever dreamed of is that you have goodness and determination to give something back to others.

As your blessings pour in, bless others and give to those who are less fortunate. Spread the words of love and power to others. Help others realize that they, too, can achieve their dreams. Your success will be the ultimate demonstration that **GOOD PEOPLE REALLY CAN WIN!**

Five Steps That Guarantee Success
●●●●●●●●●

Success is not difficult to the men and women who develop a success mentality and have the courage to follow their visions. Can the information and strategies in this book guarantee success ? YES, YES, YES!! But you must take action; start today!

With the information you've received so far, you now have all the tools you will ever need to create a successful life. But we can do more to enhance your opportunities. Here are five more strategies that will continue to solidify your image as a difference-maker, problem-solver, a value-creator.

1) Know Thyself: Understanding Your Own Value
Most people fail to really get to know and understand themselves. Before others can learn to value and

appreciate who you are, you must learn to appreciate yourself. To do this you must learn/know who you are, and understand your value.

WHY?

The only way you can ever bring value to others is to know what things you do that are valuable. Because most of us are not very sure how we bring value to others, this confusion leaves most of us unsure about what we could achieve.

Increased knowledge of ourselves allows us to channel our thoughts, energies, and efforts into those activities where our talents can be used to provide or create the greatest benefit or outcome! Implementing those activities that provide the greatest value (i.e., product or service), enhances your own profitability, marketability, and prosperity. This is how people can increase their worth to their organization, or in their personal relationships.

How Do You Do It?

A) Immediately begin gathering information about yourself. Examine yourself mentally and do a self-assessment of the traits you currently possess. Ask yourself (and list your answers to) the following questions:

★ What am I like?—(likes/dislikes)

★ How do I respond to challenges? (what's my assessment?)

★ What traits within myself do I admire most—value most?

★ What are my greatest talents?

★ What do I enjoy doing the most? Why?

NEXT,..ask yourself:

Of those traits that I admire the most (in myself), what are the benefits I achieve when I use these traits and skills?

B) Ask others to tell you what they believe your greatest assets to be. See if your friends can tell you, in specific terms, what they think you are good at. As they tell you, continue you to ask them, "What are the benefits I gain/give through use of my talents or skills?"

There are a number of benefits associated with this activity. First, you gain a greater understanding of yourself and where your strengths lie. In addition, you learn how others perceive you and where they see your assets.

2) Keep Getting Sharper

Doing a self-assessment will provide you with the insight and direction needed to improve the outcomes you are creating. One of the truly exciting aspects of life is the phenomenon of improving. No matter where you are now in terms of professional and/or personal skills, you can get better! Begin immediately to commit yourself to "Getting Sharper!"

Getting sharper happens when one truly understands the value of life's experiences. Within these experiences are tremendous learning and growing opportunities. In fact, to the person who is committed to getting sharper, there is something to learn from every experience!

To get sharp, review every experience or happening in your life and ask the following:

1) What was the situation? (How was I involved?)

2) What was the outcome I wanted, or desired?

3) What was the outcome I achieved (through my own action/inaction)?

4) Was the outcome exactly, or close to, what I wanted? If not, why?

5) If the situation were to happen again, would my response be the same, or different? What would I do differently?

6) What did I learn?

   ★   about this situation

   ★   about the people I was dealing with

★ about myself

7) What kind of response could I implement in the future to achieve an outcome that maximizes the benefits for myself and all involved?

Getting sharp is learning to achieve the maximum outcome or benefit from every activity. This means that you are constantly looking for ways to do things better, minimize mistakes, and maximize outcomes. *This approach applies to every activity in life!*

Getting sharp is also using formal methods of education and training to enhance your ability to respond in a productive manner. It includes:

★ learning more about the various aspects and responsibilities associated with your job
★ learning the technologies, their capabilities, your response options, and the benefits associated with each option

Getting sharp provides you with a system for continuous assessment, evaluation, and learning. In short, it's your personal continuous quality improvement process!!

REMEMBER these critical questions regarding your responses:

★ Did the activity yield the outcome/result I desired?
★ What would I have to do differently to get a better outcome?

3) Continue to Bring Value to Others

We enhance our reputation by creating value in all relationships. The secret to achieving wealth lies in your ability to create value, or some benefit, to all that you associate with.

It's amazing, but most people fail to achieve a significant degree of success because they don't understand the tremendous opportunities that are present with every relationship! Most people approach their jobs and other relationships with this question, "What's in it for me?"

Of course, this is not shocking! It shouldn't be; the great majority of us feel this way. We always want to know how a situation will enhance or improve our lives. This is why I say that most people haven't got a clue when it comes to creating success for themselves. We are too self-centered and always concerned with what we can get out of a situation. *We should concern ourselves with what we can bring to a situation!*

You must understand, you get paid for what you DO! You get paid well when you do it better than others can. And you get paid very well when others recognize you as a value-creator, a producer!! This is why we keep working to improve our skills, so that we can increase our value! So, as you approach your work (or play), continue to ask yourself:

★   How can I be great at what I do?
★   What would I have to do to be excellent?

★ What jobs do I perform well now?

★ What jobs give me the greatest trouble?

★ WHAT MUST I DO TO GET BETTER, AND BETTER, AND BETTER?!

What Are Their Concerns:

As you approach others regarding a venture, an agreement, a partnership, a relationship, or a job, ask yourself: "What are their concerns?" Any time you are preparing to be involved with others and you want to enhance your value, continually speak, and think, from the other person's perspective! Try to find out their wants, their expectations, their needs—then address their needs and EXCEED THEIR EXPECTATIONS!!

Do this for all relationships—from your job to your loved ones—and watch how the respect, appreciation, and admiration others have for you skyrocket! You will be so valuable that it may only be a short time before you are promoted, compensated, or rewarded in some manner! It's truly an exciting and productive exercise!

4) You Are the Solution

Think for a moment about how businesses stay in business. If a business wants to grow and flourish, it must provide products or services that are valued by its consumers. Now, what happens to the business if its products or services lose their value in the eyes of its constituents or customers? If the constituents of a business no longer value the services of that business, then the business must do one of the following:

1) Enhance the product/service to increase the value

2) Create new products the constituents will appreciate

3) Go out of business!

Businesses then have the challenge of either continuing to get better by providing new and improved services, or by taking the risk that their current products will continue to be valued by their customers.

I mention the plight of business because of its relevance to your success. Someone once said that people should carry themselves like a business! Let's examine this philosophy further. For example, if you work for an employer, why did this employer hire you?

Now go a step farther. If you know why your employer hired you, then what kind of service or product value are you providing? Now answer this question:

> If you were an independent contractor, or consultant, providing a service to your company, would they still be buying services from you?

If you had to make it on your own as a business, doing the same things you are currently doing now (except you'd have to solicit each job from a buyer), would you still be in business?

Please understand: If you truly desire to have a happy and abundant life, you must be committed to providing the best services/products that money can buy! When a company hires you, don't see yourself as an employee doing another job, see yourself as a solution to whatever your organization needs! It's not just a job, it's our life, our profession, our reputation, our integrity, our skills and competence!

So begin immediately to see yourself, and carry yourself, as a business. This means that you will always provide high quality products or service, and you will continue to improve and enhance your personal services. Why? Because you understand that it is necessary to enhance your relationship with your employer (your customer), and it keeps your "business" profitable and growing! When you provide value, people want to do business with you. Keep getting better and better, and better...

5) Communicate, Communicate

One of the greatest, yet underappreciated, success tools available to each of us is the ability to communicate. This is such a powerful tool, it's a shame so few of us take advantage of the benefits it can create for us. I am not going to give you a lesson on communication. The only thing I'll say here is: Start telling people how you can help them!

It's unfortunate, but many people have lost the ability to communicate effectively. Too many of us spend our time talking *at* people, instead of talking *to* them. Why is communication so critical to your success? Because *we can get anything we want in life, if we know how to ask!* Here are five effective communication strategies:

1) Speak with a purpose. Anytime you are speaking to someone, quickly think of the outcome you'd like to achieve from the conversation. For example, if a friend has come to you to talk about some problem they are having, think through the outcome you want to achieve from your response (i.e., understanding, empathy, love). What is it you really want them to know? Communicate it. Always have a purpose in mind when you speak.

2) Make it plain. Keep conversations simple and to the point. Speak from their knowledge base, in their language. This way you'll know they will understand you.

3) Speak in terms of benefits. Stay positive! Let people know what you can do for them. Let them know of the services you can provide. Tell them what you need to be effective. Tell how they'll benefit from an association with you. What are the results you plan to deliver. Speak in terms of benefits and results. If someone is providing a service to you, communicate exactly how you'd like that service delivered. If you are selling a product or

service, how does it enhance their ability to meet their objectives, or attain profits!

4) Speak to their concerns first. Always address others' issues and concerns before telling others what you want. If people see that you are interested in their needs, and they see that you have options for addressing those needs, they will be happy to do business with you!

5) Listen. I know that I mentioned this in an earlier chapter, but it's too important not to mention again here. When it comes to effective listening, remember to take a sincere interest in what the other person is saying. Listen to their words, their emotions, the impact of their words, their concerns. Hear them. When you do this it puts you in a position for an effective and knowledgeable response. When you respond to them and address their concern, you will have increased your value substantially!!

These extra tidbits will enhance every phase of your life by improving the quality of your relationships. People will appreciate you and want to do business with you because of your interest in them and your determination to provide solutions!

Start immediately assessing, evaluating, and improving your response to others. Do the same with your job. Are you providing valued service? What can you do better? And remember to communicate,

communicate, communicate in a manner that shows others that you have an interest in their success and well-being! I guarantee you'll see results almost immediately!

The Single Most Important Success Builder

●●●●●●●●●●●●

Life is truly wonderful and exciting. It is fantastic living in a world without self-imposed limitations. Every day I grow stronger, more confident, and more convinced that success is mine—and yours. I hope you are enjoying yourself and having a good time.

We've discussed the systematic process for building success habits that will make you virtually unstoppable in your quest for success! Follow our success formula and get ready for action. It will happen faster than you imagined!

I can *almost* guarantee that you will be successful. Did you notice that I said *almost*? That's because there is something you must do to ensure material affluence and wealth! This activity will open doors to unlimited wealth-building opportunities. Without it, you can still achieve success, but it might be more difficult and take longer to happen. What is this activity that will bring wealth and abundance to you quicker than you can imagine?

GIVING!

It's as simple as that. *The moment you commit to giving, everything is available to you.* It is a spiritual law that giving engenders receiving! Most importantly, when you give, the return to you is multiplied. The Bible says: "Give and it shall be given to you!"

This Bible verse says it best: 2 Corinthians, chapter 9, verses 6 and 8:

> But this I say, He which soweth sparingly shall reap sparingly; and he which soweth bountifully shall reap also bountifully. Every man as he purpose in his heart, so let him give; not grudgingly, or of necessity: For God loveth a cheerful giver. And God is able to make all grace abound toward you; that you, always having sufficiency in all things, may abound to every good work.

The moment you commit to giving to others, it will be returned to you multiplied, and you will have sufficiency in all things! This is true when the giving is unconditional and from the heart. The reason you give is equally as important. When you give, it should be done to provide a sense of well-being, happiness, and love to the receiver!

Does It Work??

It's amazing that more people don't see the connection. When you observe those people who have achieved a great degree of success, have you noticed that they created that success because of their commitment to providing some service to others? Were men like Thomas Edison, Henry Ford, and Booker T. Washington successful because they were thinking only of success? Not at all. These men (and other successful giants) were able to accumulate wealth and power as a by-product of their commitment to provide (or give) some kind of worthwhile service to benefit others!

Look throughout history at those who have achieved and you'll be astounded that the great majority of those people achieved success only after they created some product or service that in some way enhanced or improved people's lives (or standard of living).

GIVING = SUCCESS IN ALL AREAS OF LIFE!

Build your success through giving. Remember back in chapter 2, we discussed how you can create self-talks, or affirmations, to build your exciting vision of the future. One self-talk that should be immediately added to your daily ritual is this one: "I am a giver!"

In addition, by committing to be a giver, you maintain your value in relationships with your employer, your spouse, your family. As you give, they will give back to you. Deepak Chopra, wrote in his book *The Seven Spiritual Laws of Success*:

> Practicing the law of giving is actually very simple: If you want joy, give joy to others; if you want love, learn to give love; if you want attention and appreciation, learn to give attention and appreciation; if you want material affluence, help others to become materially affluent. In fact, the easiest way to get what you want is to help others get what they want!

It's simple to do. Think about it. How can you increase or enhance your giving in life? Here's how it can work for you.

GIVING:

> **SELF**—Love, honor, and cherish yourself. Have a healthy respect for your value. Go after the things you truly desire. Live your life with a passion! Each day do something special for yourself.

> **JOB**—Provide more service to the customer. Assist your fellow employees. Bring joy and good cheer to the office. Volunteer for special projects. Bring enthusiasm and an appreciation for the opportunity to demonstrate your talents. Try to be the best at what you do.

FAMILY—Give more time to your children. Provide love, nurturing, guidance, and support. Show interest in their activities. Provide open arms and a listening ear. Provide encouragement and support to all your relatives. Support and take interest in family functions. Take time for parents, uncles, cousins, nieces, and nephews. Bring joy and laughter to all family gatherings.

SPOUSE—Love, support, encouragement, dedication, commitment, admiration, respect, enthusiasm, and passion—what's left?

GOD—Worship in a manner that is comfortable to you. Always give to God first, and the world is yours!

COMMUNITY—Make a difference by giving where you have an interest. Volunteer to coach a soccer team. Spend time at a home for the aged. Join reading clubs and other organizations. Have fun!

All of life works the same. Life is a series of planting seeds and reaping a harvest from those seeds. Our harvest is determined by the type of seed we plant. Plant seeds of anger, resentment, distrust, and jealousy and reap the same in prejudice

Remember a seed can only reproduce after its own kind!! Plant seeds of love, honor, trust, integrity, enthusiasm, and commitment and you'll reap the same.

Giving demonstrates your value and leads to increased opportunities for abundance to flow to you. Give, give, give, and as you open your heart to spread love, goodness, and joy through giving, you'll stop and suddenly realize that you are extremely happy!

A Final Word

● ● ● ● ● ● ● ● ●

Let's get excited! It's time for you to go live your life! I have no doubt that if you maintain your fire, desire, and commitment, you will have a great life! You know the journey won't be easy, but your positive mental attitude, persistence, and determination will see you through. Remind yourself every day that LIFE IS GOOD because you have taken control of it and you won't let yourself down!

Separate Yourself from the Pack

Limitations are nothing more than a state of mind. The things we've discussed in this book will propel you past being the "Just-So Joe" or the "Plain Jane," to a place where you will truly feel capable of doing anything! You will be unstoppable!

Your mind is like a muscle—if it's continuously trained and conditioned, it will perform at an astonishingly high level for you. You will have energy, creativity, and imagination as never before and you will achieve more than you ever dreamed possible!

There is no greater thrill than the experience of seeing your ideas and actions begin to bear fruit. You will be astonished at how quickly good things will begin happening to you. ENJOY EVERY EXPERIENCE. Enjoy these times—your life as it is now, and as it will be!

Go forth and make great things happen. Create a fantastic reality. Travel, spend quality time with loved ones, and make lots of money (if that's your goal). Always remember to maintain your focus and give thanks to your Spiritual Father! Take time to enjoy the fruits of your efforts, to enjoy the abundant life that success can bring. *You are special and truly deserve all that you achieve!!*

Always Give Thanks

Remember where your blessings come from. Always give thanks to God and He will direct you and keep you.

New Culture

The most exciting aspect of your success will be that YOU DID IT. You took it upon yourself to go out and make a better life for yourself. You will take the abilities God has given you, and you will excel because you believe you can! You have rejected the "loser" image others in society have tried to place on you. Now you're ready to make it all happen. *Isn't this the ultimate challenge?*

Now you can take the message of success to others. Give another person this book. Help teach others the importance of having a vision for themselves. Teach them how the mind is the key to their success and internal happiness. You can help build a positive new culture based on strength of character and goodwill toward your fellow humans—a culture that will turn off the TV and turn on its minds for success and growth. It's all about committing ourselves to being the very best!

Finally, you will quickly learn that a happier, more spiritual person is capable of greatness. A person's mind focused on success has little time for drugs, violence, and other activities that may cause harm to oneself or to others. A person committed to success simply likes himself too much to hurt himself.

You are on your way. Get together with other strong minds and make something fantastic happen. This not only benefits you and your family, this attitude will ultimately benefit this entire country, our society, and the world. Your success will be the ultimate demonstration that **GOOD PEOPLE REALLY CAN WIN**. Life is great and the future is very bright indeed!!

COMMON SENSE LEADERSHIP

...can help you meet your personal or organizational training needs! We have a number of exciting seminar products that will provide your staff with the motivation, education, and information needed to reach their highest potential.

We can tailor our dynamic training programs to meet your specific training needs. We can also do studies to assess managerial, process, and communications effectiveness.

G. Eric Gordon is also available for retreats, keynote speeches, and other appropriate functions. Call for more information at (972) 988-3345.

ALSO...

For those of you who have trouble getting to Common Sense Leadership seminars, get valuable learning from Common Sense Leadership audio and video products. Please feel free to order any of the following (order individual products or the entire set):

1. Goal Setting Workshop (audio)	$10.00
2. Peak Performance and Creating an Exciting Vision	$15.00
3. Peak Performance	$10.00
4. Ten Steps to Greatness (video)	$30.00
Total Package	$65.00
Special!!	$49.95

To order additional copies of *Common Sense Solutions For Success*, please send a check or money order for $9.00 plus $2.00 shipping to Common Sense Leadership.

For seminar or product information, write to:

Common Sense Leadership • P.O. Box 6106 • Arlington, TX 76005
(972) 988-3345

If ordering products, please send check or money order payable to Common Sense Leadership.

About the Author

As a consultant, G. Eric Gordon brings excitement, spirit, energy, humor, and enthusiasm to every presentation! He founded **COMMON SENSE LEADERSHIP**, a consulting firm, to address personal and organizational success from a *"Common Sense—People First"* perspective. Eric believes that his mission in life is to help people live to their highest potential." An exciting, dynamic, and motivational speaker, **G. Eric Gordon** has provided quality training for organizations and individuals throughout America and the United Kingdom.

My goal is to teach people how they can do it! Anything they truly believe they can do. It took me a while to understand this principle of believing myself, but once I knew what I truly wanted, I was able to get it! What is very exciting about success is that it doesn't have to be complicated. This book, *Common Sense Solutions for Success*, is very easy to read. It's easy to understand. Most importantly, these principles are easy to apply to your everyday life.

While he grows in stature as a management and personal success consultant, Eric continues to be committed to helping individuals achieve success. Be sure to look for his next book, *The Young Man's Success Training Manual.*